If Your Head Can't, Your Heart Will . . . But What If That's Broken Too?

By Mariana Maniscalco

Baby Coop Publishing, LLC

BABY
COOP
Publishing, LLC

Rights and Permission: babycooppublishing@verizon.net

The author and publisher specifically disclaim any and all liability arising directly or indirectly from the use or application of any information contained in this publication.

Publishing Coordinator: Karen Sharp-Price
Graphic Artist: Mark Krawczyk
Permissions: Mark Mulville, The Buffalo News

Library of Congress Control Number: 2014942997

Baby Coop Publishing, LLC West Seneca, NY
www.babycooppublishing.com

Publisher's Cataloging-in-Publication Data
provided by Five Rainbows Services

Maniscalco, Mariana.
    If Your Head Can't, Your Heart Will— But What If
That's Broken Too? / Mariana Maniscalco.
        pages cm
    ISBN: 978-0-9886101-8-7 (pbk.)
    ISBN: 978-0-9886101-9-4 (e-book)
    1. Life change events. 2. Cerebrovascular disease—
Patients—Biography. 3. Catastrophic illness.   I. Title.
RC388.5 . M345 2015
616.8`10092—dc23
                                        2014942997

Manufactured in the United States of America

For my support team,
which is the size of a small country.

CONTENTS

Chapter 1   First Day of Awesome

Chapter 2   It's Just the Flu

Chapter 3   Admitted

Chapter 4   Body Slammed

Chapter 5   A Not-So-Elegant Ball Gown

Chapter 6   Drop-Kicked

Chapter 7   Have a Little Faith

Chapter 8   The Dog Days Are Not Over

Chapter 9   I Just Want to Be OK

Chapter 10   Is This Real Life?

Chapter 11   Light at the End of the Tunnel

Chapter 12   More Than a Miracle

Chapter 13   New Beginnings

Chapter 14   No, Thank You

Chapter 15   The Last Fall

Chapter 16   Nothing by Mouth

Chapter 17   Nurse Nancy

Chapter 18   Finally, a Lucky Break

Chapter 19   Goodbye Keppra

Chapter 20   Little Superman

Chapter 21   When Life Hands You a Stroke

Chapter 22   Here Comes the Sun

Chapter 23   Home

PREFACE

I was stuck in a nightmare. My blood was boiling at a thousand degrees. I had what felt like two big cereal bowls in my stomach. I could hear so many noises, it seemed like I was surrounded by a combination of fire alarms and slot machines. The left side of my body felt completely gone. I was lying in my own urine, waiting for somebody to come help me. Bugs were starting to gather on the ceiling. All of this was happening, and I wanted to scream a scream that crackles into a flood of tears. But I couldn't, because I wasn't breathing. A humungous tube was breathing for me. It made me feel like I wanted to gag up my intestines. All I knew was I was confused. Unbelievably confused. Just below the monstrous ruckus, I could hear a familiar noise. It was the noise of typing computer keys. It was my dad, and just then, I thought there was hope, that this was really just a bad dream. My dad is here, and I can go home any minute now. I can go back to life as I always knew it.

Unfortunately, I had forgotten that I was still hooked up to those miserable machines, the left side of my body was still MIA, and my body still felt like it was boiling in hell. I couldn't speak, so that was out of the communication picture. I waved my right arm, motioning to my father that I wanted to write with a pen.

When he brought over a sheet of paper, it took every ounce of my strength to scribble out two words: *What happened?*

If Your Head Can't,
Your Heart Will . . .

But What If That's
Broken Too?

CHAPTER ONE
First Day of Awesome

It was the first day of high school. I obviously was ready well before the time I needed to be. What girl wouldn't be? The promise of hot boys, more freedom, and driving were starting now. (Well, not the driving part quite yet, but soon enough.) My first day of high school was here. My first day of something I have never experienced before. When I got to school, I soon realized that this wonderful place also meant a whole lot of new, not-so-wonderful responsibilities.

After the first three days or so, I got hit with a not-so-spectacular reality. The girls were prettier, their outfits were cuter, the boys weren't any classier, and the work was harder. I mean, please. Does anyone even care about the fertile lands of Mesopotamia, or the way a fat molecule is composed?

In reality, high school isn't how it is in a Disney movie. Thank you, Zac Efron, for screwing up my perception of high school. All of us are not in this together. High school is more like a place where everyone goes, don't notice anything around them, and goes home.

Nevertheless, to me, high school is important. Ask the majority of the kids at my school if schoolwork is important. Some will say yes, because their parents tell them that it is. Get good grades, get into college, get a good job. This might be true. But most people don't put two and two together. High school is a place where we have to test out stuff we like and don't like, find out the things we're good at and things we're not good at. I don't mean to sound like an adult trying to sell a load of crap off to their students, but this is what I believe. After high school, you're thrown out into the "real world," as some might say, where there is no extra credit or people who will cut you slack and wait until you're ready. The world will not stop rotating on its axis (learned that in Earth Science. At least I remember something.) just so you can catch up. High school gets you ready for life. When you graduate, some people consider it a release from a jail that resembled hell. You're an adult ready to leave the nest and fly on your own path, and it only crosses with your parents' path occasionally. (Well, unless your passion is to become a rookie wedding DJ and live in your parents' basement your whole life.)

Nobody ever said life is easy, but you're not going to get anywhere sitting on the couch watching Judge Judy and eating salt and vinegar chips. If school does not come easy, that does not give you an excuse to give up. It gives you a reason to try harder and disprove any doubts about you.

CHAPTER TWO

It's Just the Flu

Overwhelmed. That's the word to describe that night. I was physically, emotionally, and mentally exhausted. I was almost failing science, the boy I really liked was inconsistent and confusing, and my grandma was sick and on the verge of death. I was going to explode. What? It's not bad enough that we have science every day for 45 minutes, and there needs to be a class on learning the parts of the microscope with a lab partner you don't know or like? I just wanted to sleep for a week, not talk to anyone, not do anything, and just sleep as soon as I hit my pillow. The next morning, my throat felt like it was ripped open with sandpaper, and not the usual brace-face, canker-sore rip-up. It was no average-Joe sore throat, because while the pain was worse, there were no other symptoms. No runny nose, no cough. I figured it was from the stress. After my minor melt-down in my room the night before, there was no way I was planning on going to school like this. So I didn't go to school that day for all of those reasons combined.

Missing school didn't help the stress level, no matter how many episodes of trashy reality TV I saw. Sitting on the couch watching stupid criminals, divorce court, bratty beauty-pageant toddlers, and, of course, the classic "my mother slept with my brother-in-law" crap, I could almost feel my brain cells combusting. I was stuck eating Ramen noodles and watching garbage for almost 24 hours straight.

The next day, I was still completely and utterly sick, lying in the bathroom with my stomach to the floor. I was so very, very cold, I thought I was going to die of hypothermia in a 70-degree house. My body went into rapid, seizure-like, erratic shivering. I mean, this wasn't just the blue lip, get-out-of-a-cold-pool-on-a-windy-day type of shivers. I was almost convulsing. When you're freezing, you do everything you can to get warm, right? So I filled the bathtub and got in. Bad decision. I just felt a gazillion, trillion times worse. That was totally unacceptable. Then I started vomiting every couple of minutes. We decided to go to the pediatrician's office. My dad took my throw-up bowl, my blanket, and me and carried it all into the car. The only problem was that my dad is a human compass. We call him that because he always says he knows where he's going, but he has a horrible sense of direction. And the pediatrician's office moved to a new location out in who knows where.

So we drive around for more than an hour and we finally get there. Success! My dad carries everything in—me, the blanket and all—and plops me in the waiting-room chair. The receptionist asks my name and tells us we're not on the list. We are at the wrong doctor's office! How does that even happen?

After packing everything back in the car, we set off to the actual office, just down the road. When the doctor called me in, he had a look of confusion on his face. I told him everything that was going on, and all he said was that it definitely wasn't the flu. He ordered blood work and told me to drink fluids and try to keep my body cool. Other than that, he knew as much as we did. This was all so confusing, not to mention scary.

On top of this hot mess, I got home only to find out my nonny passed away. It was extremely hard, but I didn't even have the option to mourn. I felt like I was being so inconsiderate and selfish by not going to the wake or the funeral. But I couldn't go. My fever was still 104 degrees, and the blood work was coming up negative. Part of me felt like I was making everything up and was going insane. The fever was ALWAYS there, hammering me. I mean, it was a hit-your-head-on-concrete, hammering headache. I had nausea that would come and go. I've always heard pain is just a mental thing, so I felt like this was a load of bologna I was making up. Nothing made sense, and at one point my mom even thought she was catching what I had. After a few days, we decided to go to the doctor's again.

This time I felt more optimistic than the last. We saw a different pediatrician, Dr. Steven Lana, and I could tell he wanted to get to the bottom of it like I did. I lay down on the little table looking at the kid-friendly characters on the wall listening, while my mom gave him the run-down on my case (which I never expected would still be a case at this point). Advil and Tylenol had lowered my fever. The vomiting seemed to come and go. So Dr. Lana did what most doctors do, a hands-on evaluation. Check the neck lymph nodes, push on the liver. When he got to my liver, he pressed really hard and dug his fingers in like my brother would do to my leg to agitate me. I told him it hurt, and it turned out he wasn't even pressing hard. That meant I had elevated liver enzymes, but he didn't know exactly what that meant yet. I was happy to hear that at least we were getting somewhere with a diagnosis.

Then Dr. Lana checked my heart. I didn't think anything of it. Duh! It's still beating, and my blood flows like a champ. It runs faster than a kid toward an ice cream truck. Wait. What is that look on his face? He pulled the stethoscope away only to put it back on to check again. It automatically felt billions of times colder. Was my heart not the champ it has always been? It can't let me down now. I'm young. When Dr. Lana finally finished his check-up, he told us he heard a murmur. *A murmur?* No, that's not possible. I had only heard that disturbing word used on the animal rescue TV shows and in the news about a boy who dropped dead during a sports game. It's funny, the worries that pop into your head. I wondered: Does this mean that we have to mark that box "yes" on the nurse's forms for the beginning of the school year? This would prove to be the least of our worries.

CHAPTER THREE

Admitted

Dr. Lana ordered us to call the hospital to schedule an echocardiogram, which is like a sonogram of the heart. All this commotion made me hungry, so I convinced my mom to take me to my favorite taco place. When I got home and ate my nachos deluxe and chicken fajita while watching *Boy Meets World*, the food didn't go down well. It felt like it was stuck in my esophagus. That made me really nervous. While I was nervous in one room, my mom was nervous in the other. She was calling Children's Hospital to make an appointment. The soonest they could fit me in was three days. This wouldn't be the first time Mom wouldn't take no for an answer. She started crying on the phone and convinced them to get us an appointment the next day.

We called my Aunt Jennifer, who works as a nurse at Children's Hospital, and asked her to go with us, because we were such hospital amateurs. I was never at a hospital for myself for any reason. Not even for a broken bone or because a popcorn kernel got stuck up my nose (which, believe it or not, caused my brother to be rushed to the hospital one time). This visit, I hoped, was going to be about getting in, finding out what's up and getting the hell away from there.

The first thing I noticed about the hospital was the smell. Like any hospital, but especially this one, it smelled like they were trying to keep the sick kids a secret. Keep their smell away behind the strong scent of rubbing alcohol and floor cleaner. We got to the echocardiogram exam room. I had to put on one of those weird tie hospital gowns and lie on a high table with a paper cover and a plastic pillow.

The exam technician, Sandy, squirted this cold, clear bluish gel that smelled like baby lotion on my chest. Honestly, it was so gross. Then she took an even colder roller ball and rolled that on my chest. On a computer screen next to the table, I watched what looked like a fishy mouth open and close with a whooshing air noise - whoosh, whoosh, whoosh, whoosh. The screen lit up in blues and reds brighter than the floats in a Disney World night parade.

I tried to read her face. What did it all mean? Was this a good or bad thing? I asked her, "How's it looking?"

She said something like, "It's reading well." They're not allowed to tell you anything. Only the doctor can give the diagnosis.

Aunt Jen suggested we go down to the emergency room and wait for the doctor there. My temperature was still 104, and Aunt Jen said I looked "ghoulishly gray." The emergency room area where they put us, looked nothing like what I imagined it would. It was definitely not *Grey's Anatomy* in there. There were no bloody stretchers getting rushed from one end of the room to the other. It was surprisingly calm. It really never occurred to me that emergency rooms could have a calm day. I thought they were always in a "state of emergency." It had a table-like bed and two chairs. I was exhausted and starving.

I lay on that hard table-bed with the plastic pillow that I hated and will always hate. I asked my mom for food but she was in no mood to leave me there. So she flagged someone down and got some animal crackers and apple juice. Not exactly Mighty Taco, but it will do, I thought. My dad was out of town on a work trip, so my mom had to call in other back-up support. Who better to call for back-up than Aunt Lisa?

Whoa, if you don't know Aunt Lisa, trust me, you're missing out on life. Aunt Lisa comes in a room like a storm. Not a bad type of storm, more like a rush of warm air and hot, sunshine love. She's a kindergarten teacher and brings the enthusiasm, 24-7. She can lighten any type of mood or situation. She shows gratitude to everyone. She would meet a nurse and say, "Thank you, Mr. Bill," stressing every syllable to make them feel special. It was good to have Aunt Lisa around for moral support.

Finally, the cardiologist came in. His name was Dr. Joseph Orie, and he was the definition of good bedside manner. He wore a fun, comic-character tie and was very handsome. I immediately nicknamed him Dr. Cutie-pie. You can see the nurses swoon whenever he walks in the room. Dr. Orie delivers the truth very accurately and with a teaspoon of hope. So he told us what was going on in the most hopeful way possible. The diagnosis was mitral-valve regurgitation. There were little deposits of unknown substances on my heart valve, which were causing the valve to not open and close perfectly. Basically, blood was leaking the wrong way in my heart because of the deposit on the valve. I thought to myself, I can't wait to go home after this. I'm so tired. About ten minutes later, a different nurse came in and told me that they were keeping me in the hospital until they found out the cause. I had never been to a hospital, and now I had to spend the night—or who knows how many nights? I was so scared.

CHAPTER FOUR

Body Slammed

When I got into my room on the eleventh floor, I was exhausted and having an attack of the freezing-cold shakes. I don't think anyone really understands how hard it is to deny your body warmth when you feel hypothermic. We figured my body was shaking because my fever was so high, and I needed to cool off. I had to lie in bed with no covers, but my fever was so high I felt worse than going into an air-conditioned building in a wet bathing suit. I was lying there like a newborn baby—cold, helpless and wanting to cry.

A doctor came in and did the exact same thing as everyone else did in the emergency room. Does it hurt here? Here? Here? I didn't understand why the heck he couldn't just get the update from the other people, but I was cooperative. When he was done, I was like, "OK, so what is it?" He said he wasn't sure. I thought, well, you better figure it out! Another doctor came in and did the same exact thing! This one didn't know, either. After that, a whole wave of young doctors came in while one doctor pushed on my stomach, speaking loudly to them all. They all started to cluster over to me and do exactly the same thing! 1, 2, 3 ... 8, 9, 10 ... 13, 14, 15 doctors! Here? Here? Here? It took all I had to not say, "Stop

touching me." My mom, being the boss she is, got them all out in
a nice way and told them I am not their class demonstration. It was
almost Halloween time, so I watched one Halloween movie after
another with my mom's iPad. Trust me, it was so boring. Eventually, I met Dr. Howard Faden, the head of the infectious disease
department at the hospital. He was an older, nice, friendly man,
and he became one of my favorites.

He updated my mom on my blood cultures and told her that
the only thing that was growing in the cultures was the Haemophilus bacteria. It's a bacteria that is on your skin and in your mouth
all the time, and normally does no harm. This usually only shows
up if they don't clean off your skin well enough when giving you
a shot. It also takes longer than most cultures to grow. The doctor
asked me all these crazy questions like if I drank unpasteurized
milk. I had no idea what he was talking about. He explained that
it was milk straight from a cow udder, and I just looked at him
and laughed. Who would do that? Eventually they came to the
conclusion that it was from the movement of my teeth that had
heavy-duty braces on them. Somehow, the bacteria got into my
bloodstream and was causing a problem, which is an extremely
rare occurrence —like more than one in a million—even for someone with braces. I was going to be put on heavy intravenous antibiotics. Specifically, I was on Vancomycin, but when they started
running the bag of medicine into my arm, my head got very itchy,
like lice. Then the lice-like feeling traveled down my neck and
eventually consumed my entire body. Apparently I was allergic to
it and would be pre-treated with Benadryl from now on to prevent
the Vancomycin from making me itch all over. My mom and dad
sat there holding my hand the whole time and never left, not even
at night.

The only thing that made it less bad, was they had great mac
and cheese. Honestly, it was so good. I would eat mac and cheese
every day, then get my IV of Benadryl (spaced out properly, be-

cause the Benadryl tended to make me drowsy). During one of the IV's, I fell asleep with the food in my mouth and the fork in my hand, which made me float on a magic cloud of bliss and sleepiness. This exact cycle lasted about three days, except on the third day my right hand began to swell like a water balloon. I couldn't even move it. They explained to me that it was just edema, a side effect of my heart not functioning fully. My two doctors put me on this pill, Lasix, which got rid of extra fluid. Dr. Orie told me that it would make me pee like a racehorse. He was right. I don't remember a lot from that night, but I remember getting up to pee a lot. I called my friend on video chat and said, "I'm really scared."

We both were about to break down in tears, but we held it together and I went to bed. I remember getting up to pee that night and being really tired.

Early the next morning, Dr. Faden showed up in my room asking me why I was so tired. I replied sarcastically, "Uh, I don't know. You tell me, you're the doctor." Wow, I always knew I was a jokester, but I never thought that I would be joking on my death bed. Apparently, I was tired because I was having a stroke, although we didn't realize it at the time.

Like I said, I don't remember much, but I was told that earlier that morning I got up to go to the bathroom. I remember thinking something was really funny and my mom was upset with me because I was laughing. It turns out that nothing was funny, but I was just loopy and laughing at nothing, and Mom was really scared. She had the nurses send for Dr. Faden. I don't remember anything else about that morning but going to sleep.

When I woke up I was really hot and panicking. I was on some sort of really hard plastic, and there was a loud humming noise. I was extremely uncomfortable, to the point where I couldn't hold still. I was tossing and turning my head left and right like the stereotypical thing you see on TV or in movies when someone is having a bad dream. That's all this was. A bad dream. I'll wake up tomorrow, and I'll go see my friends at school, I thought. I felt like Augustus Gloop when he got sucked up the tube of hot chocolate in *Charlie and the Chocolate Factory.* On top of feeling hot and claustrophobic, there was a huge tube going down my throat, which made me extremely nauseous and made me gag. After what felt like an eternity, I felt the plastic beam move out of the tube. I was in a CT scan tube. The doctors were having my brain scanned to see how big of a stroke I had suffered. I was frail to the point where I wasn't thinking straight and couldn't say anything when I got out of the tube. I saw a familiar family friend, Dr. Marino, who happened to be the anesthesiologist for the test. He said, "She's gonna give me gray hair," which didn't make sense to me because he already had gray hair. Apparently, he needed more anesthesia than he expected to keep me still. They put this big, blue, plastic-smelling balloon over my nose and mouth, and I was thinking, "Hey, how the heck am I supposed to breathe?" But they squeezed the balloon and then the smell of a strawberry patch came across me and all the lights went out. What the heck? They gave me some sort of strawberry opium air.

CHAPTER FIVE

A Not-So-Elegant Ball Gown

When I woke up, there was a really pretty, young nurse standing over me. She told me her name was Catie. I'm not positive how it is spelled because of the amount of drugs that were whipping through my bloodstream at that moment. She looked like Taylor Swift. We should hook her up with my brother Ben, I thought. (He loves Taylor Swift.) I told her I liked her earrings, and she told me she got them from Forever 21. We had a whole conversation about Forever 21, because thinking about anywhere other than the hospital was a comforting escape and helped reinforce I was still me, deep inside. Underneath the vast mountains of tubing surrounding my body, there still was the same fashion-loving, light-hearted, hilarious (not to toot my own horn, but I am) girl inside somewhere.

After a lot of thinking, I finally built up the strength and courage to ask where I was. They told me I was in the PICU. Ouch, I thought, that sounds painful. The PIC part of it made me think of an ice pick or the phrase, "prick me with needles." I was in the Pediatric Intensive Care Unit, but I couldn't even describe the area

I was in as a room. It was more like a dark, designated piece of flooring. I was in a plastic hospital bed with sheets that obviously were not the 400-count I was used to and beyond missing at that point. The pillow also was plastic. There was a broken reclining chair, a tray table and a tiny TV that definitely was there since before 1992. This all was contained behind extra-thin, hideous, pastel, pink and yellow cloth curtains with seashells and some sort of leaves printed on them. Like, who would choose that? I always thought about being a designer, and even with zero training I knew that they were ridiculous, especially considering they were zero-percent efficient at keeping the noise from beeping machines out and privacy in. Every few minutes or so, imagine a pounding so loud, that it's like someone is beating the dust out of a rug with all their might. Boom, boom, boom, boom, boom. I asked my Aunt Jen what that was and she told me it was for children who need to be patted on the back because they had pneumonia. All I can say is, I'm happy that booming sound wasn't echoing through my chest cavity.

My mom came over and told me I had a stroke. *A stroke?* Only old people have strokes. I remember this from when I used to go to physical therapy with my grandma. I used to look at those people like they were such foreigners. How could one side of their body work and not the other? It turns out the stroke hit the right side of my brain, which affected the movement of the left side of my body. At that point, the left side of my body still worked, but felt pretty heavy.

I was in a weak spot, like a baby who is new to the world, just placed on the measuring table, cute and vulnerable. When people tell me I'm cute (like in a childish way), I usually just give them a dirty look, get offended and talk in my adult-maturity voice. When dealing with many of the girls my older brother brings over to the house, I decided this was a losing battle. "Aww, she's so cute, how old is she?" they all would ask.

My brother would joke, "She's not cute."

The girls would flirt back with him and try and get on my good side by saying something like, "Aww be nice, Mike," in a ditzy, air-headed voice, for which I had no patience.

However cute I might have been at this moment, I sure had no patience for it. My mom came in, and I told her, reasonably, that I had to pee. I asked where the bathroom was. But to my ultimate defeat, she told me I couldn't get up, and that they were going to put something called "hospital pants" on me. I said, "Heck no, there is no way that I am wearing a diaper," which was exactly what they were. I eventually agreed, because there is nothing more accurate than, when you've got to go, you've got to go.

After a lot of fussing to keep all males away from my curtained area, they put it on me. As I lay there in my diaper, I felt that not only was my body wounded, so was my ego. I could feel my soul slipping out of my body. I was turning into a sick-kid shell, where you look like yourself but the shell of your body is really all that is left, along with all your memories of better days. To escape from this feeling, I went onto Facebook to feel still in the loop, considering that's where the whole teenage population posts its every moment of life, play-by-play.

What I saw made me sink even deeper into my shell of a self, sitting in a diaper in a hospital gown. That night was the homecoming dance at my high school. I was supposed to be there. I should be putting on a super-hot dress, curling my hair, doing my makeup and having the time of my life. This made me so upset. At that moment, I would have given anything to be there. Just then, they ran who-knows-what through my IV, and I soon was more loopy than a drunken sailor on a Ferris wheel. The bits and pieces I remember, are the nurse giving me blood and saying my lips look so pink, they should make a lipstick that color. I liked the transfusion of blood so much because I could feel it regulating my body temperature. I found myself just saying, "Blood. I want blood, please," to the nurses. I remember picking at the diaper I was trapped in and getting yelled at by my mom, which never happens because I never make her that upset. (She was already on edge, like any mother would be.)

So much for the night of my first homecoming dance.

CHAPTER SIX

Drop-Kicked

The next thing I remember is waking up in a daze. I had a trachea tube down my throat. I couldn't talk. I thought the dots on the plasterboard ceiling were bugs, and there was something unbelievably foreign in my abdomen. It felt something like the big, round plastic bowls we use in our house for cereal. I was extremely frightened and confused, considering I couldn't talk. I did what my friends and I used to do in middle school when the lunch room got in trouble and we had to be silent. I lifted my right hand, thumb index and middle finger together, and moved it up and down in little waves to mimic a pen. That's when my dad held up a paper and I scribbled out, "*What happened?*"

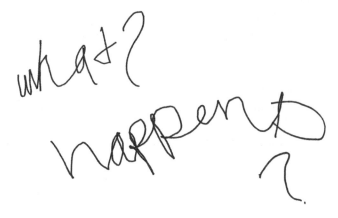

My dad explained to me that they were keeping me heavily medicated. He talked on and on, more than necessary, and finally told me the doctors had put two pieces of my skull in my stomach. I knew I had a bandage on my head. I could sense that what was in my stomach was a very hard, large bone. I wrote on the paper he was holding up, "Obviously."

What actually happened, was three days after my stroke, my brain swelled up and I had what is called a hemorrhage, which is bleeding in the brain. They had to do an operation and put one piece of my skull in my stomach to give the brain room to swell up. Three days after that, I had a brain aneurysm. The bacteria—Haemophilus—had lodged on my heart valve. Every time my heart beat, it sprayed tiny bits of bacteria through my body. The bacteria had clumped in tiny spots in my brain to cause the initial stroke. More of the bacteria had clumped in an artery in my brain, causing a blockage that burst. My Aunt Jennifer, the nurse, happened to be in my hospital room visiting me the moment it happened. She could see my eyes roll up in my head and my breathing stop. She put an oxygen bag on my face and kept me breathing. I was rushed into an operating room, and two brain surgeons performed another major operation. They took another piece of my skull off and put it in the other side of my stomach. Then they put a coil, like a plug, in the burst artery in my head to stop the bleeding. They cleaned out the blood that had leaked into my brain and bandaged me up. I nearly died on the way to the operating table.

The doctors kept me almost totally unconscious, in a drug-induced coma, for about a week. I finally woke up to my family members around me and an extreme burning sensation on my head. I reached to touch it but there were tight bandages around my head and my ears were wrapped in it. They kept the two big pieces of my skull in my stomach to keep them fresh. If they kept them frozen, they'd get "freezer-burn," like old frozen food in the refrigerator. My head burned and itched so bad that I wanted to rip off all the bandages and give it a huge scratch. It was way worse than when you have an itch on your back that you can't reach. The most obvious thing to do was to rip and tear at the bandage. When it finally started coming undone, my mom came over and scolded me like I was a little kid and said, "If you keep doing that, they're going to tie your hand down."

I just replied, "Then tie it down." I didn't respond like that because I was trying to disobey, but I couldn't help but try to be rid of that burning itch. I was basically asking her to tie it down, because I couldn't help myself. Sure enough, a little later that day, they tied my right hand to the side of the bed. I also saw bugs crawling all over the ceiling because of all the narcotics I was on.

My body was so hot, I asked my mom for a "hillbilly" treatment. What's that? Get ice packs and rub them on the hot parts of your body. For some reason, it made me think that this is the way hillbillies stay cool in the hot summer if they don't have air conditioning. I made up jokes like this because comedy is often my approach on everything … except at funerals and the airport, because people there really do not want to laugh. The attitude of my mom and me in this situation was, "If we're not laughing, we're crying." But honestly, we really didn't get in any laughs at all. We were forcing smiles to keep us from crying.

CHAPTER SEVEN

Have a Little Faith

Having religious faith as a teenager has never been easy, but especially in 2014. A lot of teenagers don't think much about God. Their brains are plugged into technology and they're comfortable there. Being Roman Catholic, my family always tried to go to church every Sunday. My brother and I had gone to religious education since kindergarten. I've always kept my relationship with God and strongly believe in heaven.

My father, Anthony Maniscalco, passed away before I started kindergarten. When people die, it seems as if we think of them as a better person than they actually were. Or that you loved them so much just because they're gone. I promise this is not the case with my father at all. He lit up a room as soon as he walked into it. It lit up into laughter, because he would start making jokes right off the bat.

He wasn't book smart. He was a salon owner and hairdresser. I remember him being the nicest, kindest man—a person who was close with everyone. My mom's friends would tell me that people went to him for a haircut, but they left with much more than that. He made everyone's day in the whole salon. Nobody left unhappy.

Most of all, he was the love of my mom's life. They grew up together. Their parents (my grandparents) had always been friends as well. Most of the things I know about my father, I've only heard second hand, but I know they're no exaggeration. Every story is consistent and proves the same point of how wonderful and funny he was, and how my brother and I are like him. It's not possible for anyone who knew him to get sick of the stories.

When he passed, we knew there was nobody who could ever replace my father. My dad has always been with us, watching over us since the day he passed. A few years later, my mom met a man named Mark, who was really nice. He was automatically what we needed, sent by God with my dad's blessing. He does not replace my father, he is just *another* father. We know how lucky we are to have had two great fathers within the course of our lives. Some people don't even get one.

Some people may think of my dad passing away as the worst thing that could have happened to me. I am not going to say it wasn't hard, but it really was also a huge learning experience. From my father, Anthony, I learned to live a life that you would be happy with when you're gone. And don't let the way people remember you be a stretch of the truth. Be the best person that you can be every day. Having Mark for a father has showed me that you don't always have to compare everything in this world. You can just accept things as two different people or experiences that you love.

It was still dark in my room, so I had no reference of time or how long I had been in this nightmare. You know how you can have one of those rainy, crappy, sad days where it makes you want to cry and listen to sad music? Well, every day was worse than that.

But really, all I needed was to see the sun. For some reason in the PICU, there were almost no windows, and the lights never changed. Days faded into nights with no recognition of which was

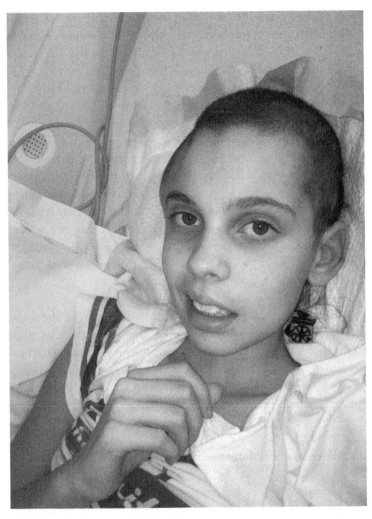

which. At that moment, I felt there was no more purpose for me on earth. I just wanted to die. I prayed to God that if He was going to have me die, that He would take me then and there, because the world no longer felt like a place I wanted to live in. Life is not about lying in your own urine getting poked at. There should be more to look forward to than an occasional sit-up in the broken recliner chair for a sponge bath or to look out the window into a cold winter's snowy, gloomy day. I was like a fish in a fish bowl looking out, waiting, wishing, wanting, needing to be on the other side of that glass. At that moment, lying there on those hot sheets that felt as if they became one with me, I saw every dream I ever had dissolve away into hopelessness. I always wondered: Who was I going to marry? What job was I going to have? Which busy city was I going to live in? What great things would I accomplish in my life? There was no future for me. I'm going to die here and be remembered as the girl who got the short end of the stick and fought strong, but inevitably lost. My life felt like it would always be inside that hospital bed or chair, contained between those four curtains forever. I had entered the hospital at 97 pounds. I was down to 75, and knew that if some other setback were to happen (even a little one), I was done for. There was no hope. I was waiting to die, counting down the minutes until my suffering was over.

My faith was being tested.

CHAPTER EIGHT

The Dog Days Are Not Over

I had what felt like one of those abnormally large pencils that kindergarteners use, up my nose. It was a feeding tube with a piece of masking tape holding it in place, and it was poking me in the eye. The nurse on duty at the time was an old and crabby lady with an old-fashioned way of nursing. She said, "Don't you dare touch that tape," and she wrestled my hand as I was trying to adjust it. All I wanted to do was move it out of my eye. Then she gave me morphine to swallow, even though I had a feeding tube going down my throat. She squirted the foul, disgusting, bitter liquid down my throat and left me with my Aunt Lisa, who watched me choke and gag on it. It made my eyes water. It could be that she put it down my throat to wean me off of the feeding tube. But she should have just communicated and listened to me, instead of looking at me with an expression that said, "No way in hell will she remember this. She's so out of it I'm going to do what's easiest for me." She could have saved me a lot of stress. She was the worst nurse I ever had. Apparently, she was there on tenure, because it sure as hell wasn't because she was kind, loving and fantastic at her job. The one day I had her, it was like I was a patient in a torture hospital like you see in those scary movies. It was unreal. You are 100 percent at the mercy of the nurse who's assigned to you.

CHAPTER NINE

I Just Want to Be OK

I woke up to something really stinky and someone saying my name. It was my brother, Michael, who was breathing on me. He was lying right on top of me in bed, saying, "Bay-bee." I don't know why, but it was our form of communication. While I couldn't speak much, he wanted me to repeat it. At this point, my dignity was so far gone, I did it. In that moment as I looked in his eyes, I could both see and feel the sadness inside him.

I didn't really get a chance to feel sad, so I just said, "Mom, Michael thinks I'm dying. Am I dying?" He didn't need to cry or say anything. I just knew. I was lying there with my brother snuggling me, and I started singing, *Be OK*, by Ingrid Michaelson. In that moment, I could feel how much my smart-aleck, instigating brother—who would take any chance to tease me—really loved me.

He looked at me and said, "We're going to get through this because you're strong." I didn't feel strong, All I have done since I've been here is lie in bed and pee in diapers. This touching moment didn't last long, because shortly after I could feel my brother blow his disgusting breath into my face—with love, of course.

So I responded, "Mom, make Michael get off of me!" Brothers. You can't live with them, but more importantly, you can't live without them.

CHAPTER TEN
Is This Real Life?

The rules of the outside world don't really apply inside the walls of a hospital. For example, you have all the free time you want and can use it doing anything. But time will never really be yours, because you're mostly stuck in bed. The food is not enjoyable. Lying in bed isn't as cozy as it looks. In fact, I rarely got any sleep. Then there's all the medicine, which is not as tasty as the cough syrup you buy at Walgreens.

By mid-November, I had improved enough to move out of the PICU and to the ninth floor. There was something oddly peculiar about it. It was quiet. Too quiet. Actually, it was the perfect amount of quiet, without the beepers and honkers to disturb me. The room was nice because it was actually a room, not a curtained-off area.

What will I do with all this time? I asked myself that question every day. I would lie there for hours upon hours, with no end in sight. Outside my window, I swore and still swear to this day, there were lit-up, floating pumpkins on the lake that I could see off in the distance.

Trying to fall asleep was actually harder than staying awake.

I couldn't lie on my right side because my skull was still in my stomach, and there was nothing to protect my brain from pressure if I put my head on that side. The left side of my body was numb, so I couldn't adjust myself to get comfortable. There was a pretty spectacular play room on this floor (the best in the hospital). The TV in my room was no longer appealing, so I decided to give the hospital's movie collection a try. My mom wheeled me into the room and set up the movie, *Bend It Like Beckham*.

It wasn't bad, but the movie inspired me to want to play soccer. Then I realized my legs didn't work. Nothing worked. I belonged on the Island of Misfit Toys. I started not just tearing up, but sobbing, realizing the feelings of anger, sadness, helplessness and hopelessness inside me. I had my mom wheel me back to bed and continued to sob for a good hour. Everything caught up to me in that moment. I resembled a victim of the Holocaust. I had no hair and was unbelievably skinny. I weighed a scarce 73 pounds. (I don't even think I weighed that little in the fifth grade.) My hair was buzzed to the scalp. It's not fair, I thought. I used to be pretty. "I'm not going back to school until my hair grows back," I said to my mom. I used to have friends. I'm going to lose all my friends. It's not fair.

Why did this happen to me when all the other people at my school get to use their legs and arms? I'd take one of their lives any day, I thought. My throat felt as if it turned into tense rubber from the anger and resentment. I just want to be normal! It's not fair! Why did this have to happen to me? The doctors told me this entire disaster was as rare as winning the lottery. Well, why couldn't that have happened? God, I thought. Why? Why would You do this to me? I didn't deserve this. I don't need to learn a lesson. I'm a good person!

After my much-needed, moping, self-pity sesh was over, I thought about just how lucky I actually was. I could have been

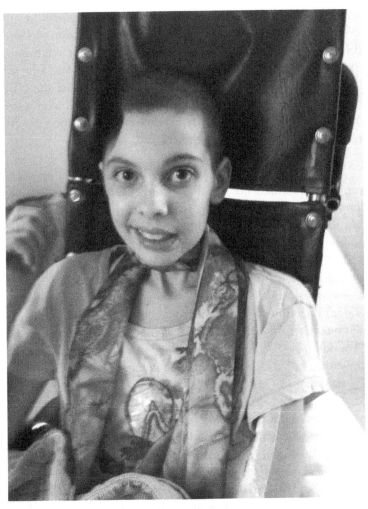

born like this, like some people are, never to know the satisfaction of walking. I could have been born a Jew during World War II and been put in a concentration camp, turn bald and skinny, be tortured and watch my loved ones die. Yes, my life might be bad, but it was not as bad as that. I have so much respect for people with physical disabilities. You don't really understand how hard it is and how much people take their health and life for granted until it happens to you. If you're the average American, just stop and think how lucky you are to have all you have and live the way you live.

As the days went on, a schedule developed. I am very blessed that my mom never left my side. She slept in the reclining chair every night (which nearly broke her back) and changed my diaper almost every time. She harassed people into doing their jobs almost every day. Every night was quite a struggle to do just about anything. Going to the bathroom was horrible. I couldn't walk so I would have to go both numbers one and two in the "hospital pants," which was unbelievably degrading.

One time while my mom was changing my hospital pants, she just looked at me and started crying. This really freaked me out because she never cries—ever. She is the strongest person I have ever met. I started to say, "Mom, don't worry about it, I'll call the nurse." I felt bad to be the cause of all this pain to everyone. I could not only see the physical fatigue, but also the emotional exhaustion in her face. I started to cry too, and I told her, "See, this is why neither of us can cry because it's a nasty cycle." But it was OK. I had my turn. It was my mom's turn now to let her feelings catch up to her. My family is stronger than I am, I thought. I slept through a lot of the most critical moments while they had to deal with it.

When my mom finally fought to get my feeding tube out, eating was a difficult task. Nothing really tasted good, considering I was going to taste it a second time when it came back up because of the nausea. Apparently, because 70 pounds wasn't healthy, I had to eat protein almost by the pound. That meant eating the most disgusting puddings, shakes and yogurts. The pudding literally came in a cat food can. My mom had to beg me to eat it. I remember throwing up my guts of chocolate, canned, protein pudding one night. It looked the exact same way coming up as it did going down.

The ultimate winner in making my stay in this horrible place even worse, was one meaningless-unless-explained word: Keppra. This one name is more evil and sabotaging than Regina George from the movie *Mean Girls*. Because I had undergone brain surgery, I was at risk of having a seizure. Actually, it was a relatively small risk. But if I had a seizure with no skull on half my head, it could have been a disaster for my brain. So they gave me Keppra, an anti-seizure medicine. There was a choice at least, between three peanut M&M-sized uncoated pills that stung like you were trying to swallow a party streamer (I don't suggest you try it), or a liquid 79 times worse than any bad liquid cough syrup. It tasted like the flavor was sour, gag-inducing fermentation. I really understand the saying "pick your poison" now, because the choice was between horrible and terrible. Most of the time, I chose the pills, smashed up into sugary, kids' yogurt. The motto in the hospital is, "Suck it up, buttercup," because you have no choice. This is what you have to do—when, where and how. Most people pity children in hospitals, but those kids are probably tougher than you are.

Every morning, I would wake up about 4:30 a.m.. Well, I would call it waking up, but I wasn't really having a deep sleep. It was more like a tortuous rest of heavy breathing. Lying there in the dark, feeling uncomfortable, because I didn't want to ask my mom for the millionth time to readjust me, I would watch the clock in the dark as best as I could until it was time to get up. If that isn't torture, I don't know what is. My life was so simple at the time. One of the few things I had to look forward to were early mornings when my mom would wheel me around the halls before the actual hall lights were on. It was dim, in-case-of-emergency lighting. This was the only time I could ever feel something that represented an in between. Every day, everything was either good or bad, yes or no, and burning-your-pupils-on or pitch-black night-time-off. This was the only time I could see in a non-florescent light. It was the closest thing to peaceful. When I was sitting up, I could breathe better. When I was lying down, my chest felt like a big elephant was sitting on it.

Then Dr. Li and this resident, Jalil, would come in and have their daily check-ins. At first, Jalil was a strict rule-follower who seemed like he only talked in scientific terms. When I first met him in intensive care, I saw that his name was Nassar Jalil, so I thought he was young enough I could call him by his first name. He seemed friendly enough, but I was on so many drugs at the time I didn't know if the name tag read last name, comma, first name. I thought his first name was Jalil. That is the evolution of Jalil's name. When I found out that I was incorrect, I liked the name so much that it stuck. Other people started calling him that, too. I viewed it as a privilege for Jalil to be called that. It was like he was Beyonce. No need for more than that one name.

Like many people I meet, Jalil broke down his aloof attitude very quickly and we became something like friends. He dropped the scientific talk around me. And I would make funny faces around him (to mock what I had to do in speech therapy, which I didn't think I needed). Eventually, he started making faces back at me when Dr. Li wasn't looking. Jalil even helped me open my markers to draw pictures when he was around. On occasion, he would even laugh at my jokes. One time on our way down for an MRI, he made a joke of his own. He asked if he should wheel my bed into the vending machines so we could get free snacks. I reciprocated with saying, "That would be stealing, Jalil." And I never heard Jalil crack a joke again. When it was time for Jalil to leave, I would say, "Peace out, Jalil," just because I could.

Many days, Dr. Li would come in and say that we were in a holding pattern, waiting until I was well enough to have surgery to put my skull back in. Holding patterns are dumb. Joke's up, Ashton Kutcher. You can come out now, I'm ready to go home, I thought. I wanted to lie on my right side so bad, it was torture. I was so sick of "seeing" my brain. The right side of my brain was still swollen. It was expanded out from my head for a good length of time and I would poke it and say it felt like a jelly fish. How many people get to say they actually felt their brain? Nobody told me not to touch it. It was horrible to look at myself in the mirror every day. I didn't see me. It didn't even resemble me. Would I ever find me? Would I ever come back? I feared I would not.

While some people my age were obsessed with their appearance—especially being desirably skinny—all I could think to myself was how stupid and overrated stuff like that was. I just wanted my body to function like it should. Speaking of legs and functioning, one time, I was lying in bed and out of the blue I noticed my left leg was huge. It literally looked like it had blown up like a water balloon. My mom was out of the room talking to the nurses at the time, but it was bigger than both of my normal legs combined. There was nothing I could do but push the nurses' button and wait. But as time went on, my overthinking habit got the best of me. I was alone, my leg was the size of Augustus Gloop's and I was scared. You're a big girl, I thought. Stop crying. You're stronger than this. Get up and go get a nurse yourself, they forgot about you. This was really just my irrationality getting the best of me at the time, but I started crying even harder. I was so scared. My mom eventually came back with my nurse. They determined it was edema, a build-up of fluid in my leg, because of my heart's weakness.

Everything was so complicated at the hospital. You can text your friends but you'll have nothing to talk about except yourself, which really isn't fun. When they ask how you are, what are you supposed to say? I'm dying? No, you say, "I'm doing good, just a couple of setbacks at the moment."

I spent many more days like these forcing myself to eat, sleep and take meds. Thanksgiving Day was spent within the walls of the ninth floor. My Aunt Paulette and Uncle Dougie Fresh flew in from San Francisco to spend it with us in the meeting room on that floor. They weren't the only ones who came. Everyone in my family came. I don't mean to sound like a cliché movie, but I realized what matters most on Thanksgiving. I never before got what it means to truly be thankful for everything. We had dinner in the meeting room. I led the Thanksgiving prayer that night. I prayed about how thankful I was for my family, and for being alive, and for the love we all share, but it was much more drawn out, thanking God for many things individually. Let's just say one box of tissues wasn't enough after that speech. That was a moment when I noticed I was still me. I was still here and not going anywhere if I had anything to do about it.

CHAPTER ELEVEN

Light at the End of the Tunnel

I started therapy every day with Mary Evans, one of the hospital's physical therapists. She was there to annoy the crap out of me until I, who felt worse than horrible, made my way out of bed. "Mariana always has more to give," she told me.

I responded with, "You know what? You're a real pain in my flaps" (like bone flaps that were still in my stomach taking up room). You never realize how heavy a limb is until it becomes unplugged from your brain and just dangles there like it's rubber. It wasn't fair. A month ago, I was capable of pole vaulting. Now I couldn't even sit up or get out of bed by myself. No one ever told me it would be this hard. My left arm would not move at all.

My occupational therapist, Dave, told me it was like trying to turn the page of a book with your mind. (Go ahead. Try it and see how it works ... Exactly.) My hand didn't work to the point I couldn't even pick up a Lego, and that made me so mad.

"One day I'll build you a Lego house and show you that my movement will come back," I said. At that point, my left hand was balled up in the tightest fist ever, 24-7. My left leg was able to move a little, but I had almost no feeling in it. With help and a full leg brace, I could stand on both feet. I could not lift my left foot at all. It reminded me of an extreme version of that Mind Flex game, where you put on a mechanical head band, and it allows you to move a special ball through an obstacle with your mind.

The problem was, I'd think so hard to try to make my left side move, and it wouldn't do anything. I couldn't even tell where my left leg or arm were in space. Too many times, my left arm would fall off the arm of a chair and dangle, or my leg would fall off the side of the bed, and I wouldn't even realize it. Whoever was in the room would have to run over and put it back. My mom would get frustrated at me for not paying attention. "Just walk," my brother would say to me, not actually trying to be insensitive. He so badly wanted me to be well.

"You don't understand," I yelled, my voice cracking, my throat tensing up and closing into what felt like solid rock. My face turned ugly and I started sobbing. (Let's face it, nobody has a cute crying face.) I could explain it a thousand different ways, a thousand different times, and he still wouldn't understand. Nobody would. I tell my left side the exact same thing as I tell my right side, it just doesn't listen. Do you understand how hard that is? I wanted to walk so badly. I wanted to feel like I had control. I wanted to feel the normality of one foot in front of the other.

To add to my long list of disappointments, I knew that when I was discharged I couldn't go home. I had to go to another rehab hospital so I could get my leg and arm working again. My mom and dad scouted out a few in-patient rehabilitation hospitals. One apparently looked like a nursing home. The Children's Institute of Pittsburgh was absolutely beautiful. It even had a pool. What I would have done to feel weightless in water. Even just a change of scenery sounded like a blessing.

CHAPTER TWELVE

More Than a Miracle

After too many days of anticipating and waiting for my head to sink back into my skull, and for my body to be strong enough, Dr. Li finally cleared me for the surgery to put my skull back in. It was long overdue. I was one step closer to me being me again.

They told me the surgery to put my skull back on my head was nothing. It was in the Neurosurgeon 101 handbook in the beginner section. Open the stomach, take out the housed skull caps that were sawed off, splice open the skin, put the skull back together, stitch it back up, and—tada—all done. Easy peasy, like your eighth-grade sewing project. I told myself I had nothing to worry about. If I had made it this far, I could deal with this too and come out whole again. I wanted to believe all I was telling myself. Nothing could go wrong, because everything did the first time. After all, I wasn't dead yet, even after a stroke, a hemorrhage, and an aneurism.

The night before surgery, my Aunt Jen, Mom and I were in charge of prepping my skin with pink soap to be extra careful that I didn't catch anything. No matter how clean they look, hospitals are the germ factories of the world. I also could not eat or drink because they were going to put a trachea tube in my body again.

They didn't want me to gag up into the tube, because then I could choke and evidently die.

The morning of surgery, my mom and family had coffees from Starbucks, and I had to ask them all to leave the room. The torture of smelling good coffee was unbearable. That morning, like all the others, we were just playing the waiting game. Waiting to live or waiting to die, just waiting for whatever was going to happen next. But today the stakes were raised because we knew it was going to happen today. I have no patience, even in good times. If you want to get on my nerves, just make me wait. Plus, I was starving. My mood was worse than a hungry, PMS-ing girl whose boyfriend just broke up with her.

Finally, a resident came in and asked us a few questions before the surgery. They were questions like what medications I was on. The man asked what side of my head I had the stroke on. I joked and said, "Really? You can't tell?" while pointing to the side of my head with the gaping dent. They rolled me down to the pre-surgery "suite." It wasn't sweet at all. It smelled sort of funny and had a lot of video games that I couldn't play because no video games were made for people who only have the use of one hand. One good thing, was everyone was there with me to take my mind off the situation. When the nurse came back, they said they were just going to pre-medicate me with some antibiotics through my IV. No big deal. After five minutes it turned into a big deal. My head started itching. Then it spread very quickly.

"Ow, ow! It burns, it burns!" I screamed. It turned out I was allergic to the medicine they were giving me, so they had to give me a different medicine to stop the itching.

They put me on an operating table. It was a harder plastic surface, which was actually a nice change of location. I lay there thinking about the possible outcomes of the surgery and it made me think about the thing people fear all their lives—death. When you're staring it right in the eye, it's not really as scary as people make it out to be. It's more disappointing to think about things that you're missing out on. The surgical prep team came in and asked me what flavor I wanted for my anesthesia. It really didn't matter. I'm going to have brain surgery, no matter what flavor it is.

The guy said, "How about blue raspberry?" The blue raspberry was really tasty, I guess. I don't even know if I was tasting it or smelling it, but I was taking it in and then—bam—darkness.

I awoke in a dream state—calm and reflecting about everything that was going on, putting the puzzle pieces together. It was a rude awakening that this was real, and I recognized the awful feeling of the PICU—the Pediatric Intensive Care Unit. It's a place where everyone is in survival mode. It's loud and chaotic. I asked if I could have lunch because I figured that's what time it was. My surgery couldn't have lasted more than an hour, tops.

I soon found out that it wasn't even the same day. I was mighty confused and sort of upset. I lost a whole day of my life that I'll never get back. Whenever I think like this, I get legitimately upset. I'll never get my freshman year of high school back. I would do anything to be that same peppy girl, bopping around with my only care being what new indie songs I would add to my playlist. I lifted up my head, with what little strength I had, enough to see my stomach. I was restricted from sitting up. I would have given so much at that moment to be back on the ninth floor. If there was one major theme to what I learned from this experience, it was that you don't know how much you have until it's gone. And that message kept coming up from behind and kicking me in all directions.

"I'm starving," I told my mom in what was probably the whiniest voice I was capable of. I just wanted to sit up and eat. I didn't want any of that cat food junk they tried to pawn off on me. I wanted *real food*, like a roast beef sandwich or a nachos deluxe with extra cheese. "Please just let me sit up," I said. "What's the big deal?" She told me I had to lie still to let the incision in my head heal.

As much as I wanted to sit up, I didn't want to get up. So when I saw the face of Mary Evans a few days later, it felt like more of a burden than a blessing. I was so unbelievably exhausted, even breathing was a burden. My leg was giant again, completely filled with fluid. How am I supposed to get up and walk in a situation like this? But they were not going to let me leave and go to the Pittsburgh rehab hospital if I couldn't walk, at least a little. My mom told me the more I showed Dr. Li how well I was doing, the quicker I would get out of this place. That was quite the ultimatum. For the first time, I got out of the dingy, plastic hospital bed with nothing but Mary Evans. I walked to the end of the hall, and all the way to the window with no aids but an AFO (ankle-foot orthotic), my running sneakers, and her little hand helping me. It wasn't smooth, but it was something. I was clunking my left foot forward, extending my knee, and holding on to her for dear life. I looked like the Tin Man when he's out of oil. It wasn't much, but I could feel a touch of hope that one day everything will be OK.

Jalil came in to my room later that night to scrub my stitches with sterile water, which was pretty painful. I said, "Jalil, do you think I'm a miracle?"

"No, more than a miracle," he said. This was special, because Jalil was a really reserved person who didn't say much. I realized how smart he was, and how he didn't think I would do what I did. This felt like a turning point to me.

CHAPTER THIRTEEN

New Beginnings

My mom and I met with Patrick Quirk, a representative of The Children's Institute of Pittsburgh. He told us everything we needed to know about staying at the CI. They told me I would have a roommate around my age and there were all sorts of kids in all sorts of conditions trying to get better. I wondered if it would be like those movies where my roommate has the exact same condition as me, and we become best friends? Or would I have a psycho roommate who murders me in my sleep? I could also go the romance-novel route where I find a beautiful boy who got screwed over like me and our experiences bring us so close that we fall madly in love, and our days spent there wouldn't matter because we were together. All these scenarios except the crazy killer roommate seemed ideal. Nevertheless, I was excited it might be a quick stay. I'd learn a few techniques and be on my way. I'd be back to school in January.

When it was time to go, they attached me to a gurney, and I princess-waved goodbye to all the hospital staff. Saying goodbye was good and bad. It meant that I was moving on, but many of those people felt like family to me. I'd miss so many of them, but their place in my life was only temporary, like many of the people I was to meet on this journey. The reason I was on a gurney was because of some dumb rule that you have to transfer from one hospital to another by ambulance. In my opinion it's a way to take more of my parents' money.

The ride was four and a half hours, but it felt a lot longer. The hard seatbelt was digging into me, and my feet felt more numb than usual because they were tightly constricted. That gurney wasn't as comfy as it looked. I felt like Hannibal Lecter under top security. One good thing was my mom brought snacks for the ride and was feeding me chips and a bottle of Fiji water. Food is definitely the way into my and most girls' hearts. It was bumpy and boring. The only thing for me to look at was all the equipment near where I was lying. The only thing I could see out of the back window was the mid-winter sky, which isn't much to look at. The only thing that kept me from complaining to my mom every second was the thought that I would go home soon.

Finally the ambulance stopped and we had arrived. Everything was so bright-colored, and everyone was so smiley. It had such a different feel than a regular hospital. A nurse gave us a tour. Every tile on the ceiling had a hand-painted design, all of them different. They explained to me that every kid paints a ceiling tile before they get discharged that gets placed up there forever.

It was just about dinner time so we went to our room. The room was a lime green, much better than the pastel room at the hospital back home. There were drawers and shelves for my clothes, a bulletin board for photos and even an up-to-date, flat-screen TV. I finally have a legit section to live in now, I thought. Then a few minutes later there was a knock on my door. The nurse brought in some food for dinner. It was turkey, mashed potatoes and corn. Real food, for me? It may not seem like a big deal, but to me this was enough to make tears well up in my eyes. Trust me, if you ate hospital food for the amount of time I did, you would have the same reaction.

The other side of my room had all the exact same things, except for the bed. There was a large bed with caged sides. It was really sort of creepy looking. Oh no, I thought, it's coming true. My roommate is crazy and is going to murder me in the night. Great, the worst-case scenario. Well, I guess we'll just figure that out later after we tour the rest of the Institute. We went into the main recreation room, and I saw something that confused me. There were all these girls walking around like nothing was wrong. One even wore a cheerleading bow. I was jealous that these girls were walking with not even a limp. They were so much prettier than me with their long hair. That probably was the thing I envied most. Why are they even here if they can walk? My mom told me that they also treat patients with a disorder called RND (Reflex Neurovascular Dystrophy), which is a disorder that triggers a painful sensation in their nerves throughout their entire body. There's no way to rid themselves of the pain. They can only cope with it by

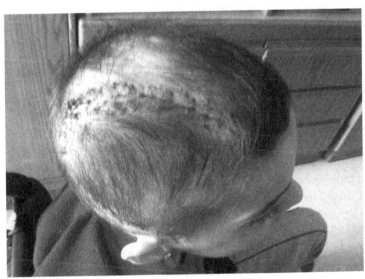

using vigorous exercise.

My coping mechanism for my appearance was rationalization. I would tell myself that other people like my short hair. I look like Natalie Portman. Boys will think it's a way to change up my look. This was to keep me from feeling truly horrible. The best thing to do was move on.

We kept looking around and there was a real lunch room with a real salad bar and too many snack choices to count. There were chips upon chips and desserts. The cashier told us as long as I was staying there I could pick anything I wanted up to eight dollars, and everything was extremely low-priced. This was like a godsend. I was 40 pounds underweight. By the time we were done touring, I was pooped, which really didn't take much.

We decided to grab dinner. I didn't get much because I still felt like poop. I was falling asleep at the table. With my whole body leaning on it, my mom was trying to convince me to finish my food but I just couldn't. I was so tired. I asked my mom to take her food up to the room because I couldn't bear to try to hold my head up any longer.

When we got back to the room it was about 6 p.m. but to me it felt like midnight. This was the first of many nearly identical nights at the CI. My mom helped me get into bed then would lie back down. Then the water pill I had to take would kick in. I would pee in my diaper, and I would have to call her to change it. We tried to use the bedside commode, but more often it was just too hard to try and get my frail body out of bed. My left leg and my left arm were dragging like a ragdoll, adding a tremendous amount of dead weight. I couldn't even pick my toes up so I wouldn't trip on them. Then my mom would lie back down on the windowsill bench (that was the closest spot near me for her to sleep), but more times than not I would have to call her back in a few minutes to readjust me in my bed. After all this, if I was lucky and didn't become nauseated and throw up like the majority of the nights, I could relax. It seemed I never genuinely fell asleep, but I relaxed my aching, swollen, broken body. I felt my lungs just pump along enough against the pressure in my chest whenever I lay down and never was able to turn my mind off, with all my thoughts and fears playing on a loop that never ended. I would lie there letting the thoughts engulf me, feeling lonely, sad, angry and bitter. When these became too bad, I just wanted to call my mom to get up again and have her hold me, comfort me, and tell me everything was going to be ok. I wasn't looking for everything to be good, I just wanted it to no longer be horrible. But I tried not to call her, because I knew she couldn't truly promise me that. There was no guarantee, no warranty, no insurance for tomorrow.

CHAPTER FOURTEEN
No, Thank You

On the rare occasions I drifted off to sleep and was lucky enough to sleep until the morning, I was woken up sharply at 8 a.m.. There was a nurse busting in my room with disgusting medicine—the Keppra, an uncoated, sour horse pill, a chalky Flintstones vitamin and two heart pills that all had to be taken on the spot under their supervision. They also would check my blood pressure with a plastic cuff. Most were pretty cold and unpleasant to begin with, but because little remained of me besides bone, getting an accurate read was quite the ordeal. It would squeeze the hell out of my arm until my hand tingled.

The thing that was really hard on me, is that I'm a relaxer. I dawdle around, do things as I feel like it and take my time. But I will always get it done. They handed me a schedule. I said, "What's this?"

The nurse said, "Your list of activities." It was jam-packed. How could I possibly do this? Someone normal would barely be able to endure this schedule. It was an activity every 30 minutes from 8 a.m. to 4:30 p.m.

I was in no mood to do any of this stuff. "Why do I have

speech therapy on here? I talk perfectly fine," I said to my mom. That was a slight exaggeration because the stroke side of my face was weaker than the non-affected side, so whenever I smiled, only one side actually lifted up. I saw this when I looked in the mirror, and I thought it looked cute—like a little kid. I didn't want to look cute. Cute gives you an inferior label. I'm in high school. I'm supposed to be going through one of those independence struggles where you close your door and tell your parents that you don't need them, listen to music they don't like, put on clothes they don't approve of and make them drop you off around the block so the hot person you like doesn't see them.

I live my life the way you jump in a pool. For a while you sit and think about it, but all that really matters is the micro-second you have of bravery to convince yourself to actually do it. Once the feeling hits you, it's not until you're mid-air that you realize what you just did. And by the time you do, it's too late. There's no way you're replanting your feet on that ledge, you're going in. The most wonderful part of this, though, is the moment you hit the water. No matter how much you like or dislike it, jumping was the better decision. No one remembers the times you didn't jump. Whenever it's a situation where I need convincing, I just think you only really regret the things you didn't even attempt.

So obviously I agreed to try my best no matter how hard it got in my therapy. I might just get better on my own, but if I try, I can get that much stronger. My dad always said, "The best you can do is the best you can do," and it always sounded too cheesy. Now I realize exactly what he meant. If you're not going to give it your all, is there any point in giving anything? I never do anything half-hearted and mediocre. Mediocrity says, "I don't care, take everything I do and make it count against me."

So early that morning, I got in my wheelchair and tried to make the best of the time I had. My mom started wheeling me to the speech room, past kids who looked like prisoners in their bodies even more than me. I tried to see them as who they really were because I know that no one wants to be seen or described by their sickness. This was extremely difficult because I didn't know them before, and I could only hope and imagine the way they would be after. Then we got to the room, I met the speech therapist and she said, "No-no-no."

My mom and I both said, "What?" She said it's a big rule that I have to wear a seatbelt while riding in the wheelchair. I scoffed under my breath because I was trying the compliant thing. My mom and I said OK, but I rolled my eyes probably pretty darn dramatically.

It felt like the whole session consisted of her testing my patience. Mouth exercises like ooo- EEEEE-ooo-EEEE's and ba-ba-ba's. The rest of the time she evaluated me but it felt like she was straight-up judging me. For example, she mentioned how I was shaking my right leg and said that it's a nervous habit. I explained to her that I'm not nervous about anything, just upset, bored and frustrated, so I get fidgety. Who wouldn't, being tied to one chair the entire day only having control of two limbs? I know she wasn't purposely doing it, but it felt like she was pointing out everything that separated me from an average healthy kid. I was trying my hardest and she was giving me test after test, which were so challenging for me to complete. They all seemed so useless and pointless, so it made me even angrier that I was doing them.

One time she had me try to put a series of statements in the proper order. For the life of me I couldn't do it. I kept running out of blanks for the letters, even though there was the same number of blanks as there was letters. I was so tired, I was falling asleep on the table in front of me. There was no way I was going to accomplish those tests (which I felt no interest in) and I felt even crappier because I got no sleep, like, ever. I was leaning off my chair again almost every day, just trying to keep eye contact. I was trapped in a place where every move, every breath was micromanaged, taken into consideration and analyzed. The only friends I had were my family members and the staff I actually liked, not that those counted as a real friendship.

When I left the speech room, I made an exaggerated point to dramatically put my seatbelt on and made one of those cool kid head nods and sang the song, *Ridin' Dirty* until we got into the physical therapy room.

The room was filled to the roof with all sorts of colorful blow-up wedges, balls, bikes, treadmills, mini-stairs and mats. It was booming with action. Most of the other children there were in worse shape than me. Many never really left their wheelchairs. I didn't really feel like leaving mine, but the thing that motivated me was that they didn't have a choice of whether or not to get out of theirs. I thought that since I could, I probably should. So I got out of my chair, but my body was so weak, it trembled with every motion. I had to carefully calculate every move I was going to make, plan every single shift in my body weight. Having a slip-up would've been so easy. I said, "OK, now that I'm up, what are we gonna do?"

The therapist said, "We're gonna play cards."

"Cards?" I said, not amused. "What's that going to do? We could play that sitting down!" She told me that standing and playing helped to build endurance and standing muscle strength. "Standing isn't supposed to be hard," I said with a crack in my voice, feeling as if my saliva had turned to solid lead. I reached for the chair. I didn't want it to be hard to walk or run or even stand! My friends are at the old, chalky gymnastics class I used to attend, whipping out round-off back handsprings. How is this fair? They can all live their lives taking everything I lost for granted. They don't understand what it feels like to not be able to move normally, to breathe normally, to have a normal body, and normal, long, flowing hair, to be what our society considers ideal.

I was doing this a lot. I'd have minor melt-downs, and that's OK. Everyone is entitled to some of those, occasionally. Deep down, I always knew that, yeah, it's not fair that it happened, especially not to me. I'm a good person. But if you think about it, nothing's fair unless you're winning some sort of award for something you did. Nothing happens to you because of how much you deserve it or don't.

God only gives you what you can handle, even if it's not what you want at all, ever. So I never actually gave up. I was entitled to put my mission on pause every once in a while. If I were to give up, I wasn't hurting the bacteria that caused this. I wouldn't have been showing the world this wasn't fair. I wouldn't have been making a point to anyone. It would have just counted against me. It would have shown the world that I was weak and a quitter. I knew it was going to take many steps and that it was going to be hard. I knew that if I didn't try I would live my whole life weak and regretting it.

In physical and occupational therapy they never asked me to do anything that was unachievable, but it was frustrating because of how totally weak my muscles were. Every simple task felt unachievable. Just stepping up one stair leading with my left leg took all my might. It would quiver and shake like I was dead-lifting 220 pounds. When I wasn't lifting it, I had to stand on it, and that was no breath of fresh air (not that fresh air would be easy for me to breathe). I was so weak, my muscles pretty much said, "Screw this, I'm not going to help," and passed the buck over to my bones. I stood with my left leg hyperextended, my bones the only thing supporting my whole body weight, most of which was water, nothing substantial. It was quite painful, but it was really the only way I could stand.

CHAPTER FIFTEEN

The Last Fall

The dreaded, painful OT and PT sessions helped me discover all the things that I definitely was no longer good at, which was a ton of things. It certainly was longer than the list of things I could do. I also had other therapies that were intended to be fun, like music therapy. The music therapist brought her guitar into my room and we sang the chorus of a song of my choice. But most of the time, because my voice was so weak, I just stood there shaking a maraca. I really enjoyed it, even though almost every day I would find myself staring off into a corner. Like I said, eye contact was hard for me, for whatever reason. My body looked lost. I had slow reaction and response times. I was like a sloth, moving slowly, talking slowly, reacting slowly. The only thing that I did quickly was vomit. For whatever reason, almost every day I would get nauseous and throw up. This seemed like a never-ending downward spiral of no sleep, forced rehab, rapid weight loss, and increased edema in my left leg and stomach.

I pushed through with everything that was necessary. I kept the same attitude that wouldn't let me give up. Never give up, I thought. You can do it. But soon, like many times, my body didn't listen to me and my wishes. I gradually became even more tired. Breathing became even more of a task. I was coughing up fluid.

When I inhaled, it made a very mucous-like crackle. Taking a deep breath was nearly impossible. I thought this was because I picked up a cold, which when living in a place with 100 other runny-nosed kids seemed more than plausible. Figuring this was all it was, my mom left Pittsburgh with my aunt to go back home to take a hot shower and get her hair cut. She needed it and deserved it. The only thing worse than wearing a diaper at my age is having to change someone my age who is wearing one.

That night my whole body felt weaker than ever before. I couldn't breathe comfortably while lying flat on the bed or even sit comfortably. Part of the problem was there were no comfy chairs. In response, we bought a mega-sized bean bag chair.

"Dad," I said, "don't worry but it's really hard for me to breathe right now. Can you just put me in the bean bag chair? It might help. And go get someone for oxygen tubes, please."

I was beyond exhausted. I would ask to go into the playroom in the Institute to sleep because I thought if I was in a different setting it would help me become more comfortable. I begged and pleaded. Please! I couldn't stand this room anymore. One thing that felt like it was getting under my skin deeper than any needle, was the question of my sanity. My life was filtered, like the people who live in North Korea. I only knew what I was told and only saw the things that happened within the walls of the hospitals I had been in. The only time I saw my house was in my dreams at night, and that was if I actually had a chance to fall into a dream state of mind. By then though, even the sweet memories of my beautiful bedroom walls, my queen-sized bed with the 400-count Egyptian cotton sheets, and my black, tasteful chandelier hanging overhead, were only in the nostalgia of my mind. They were rapidly fading. My bed sheets and pillows had been replaced by plastic and the hospital's itchy-count sheets.

My dad left while my Uncle Doug stayed and kept an eye on me to make sure nothing worse happened. My dad was taking longer than I expected. I mean, I knew the oxygen hook-up people were slow but this was sort of an emergency, and my dad should have been back sooner.

"Uncle Doug," I said, "this is getting ridiculous." Before I knew it, my dad was back with more than the same old oxygen guy, but five muscular, Grade A, hot guys. They all seemed in a panic.

"Calm down," I said, as I saw them roll in a gurney, "I just need oxygen tubes. What's going on here?" When two of the hot male paramedics embraced me (with the help of my dad and uncle) to pry me out of the bean bag chair and put me on the gurney, I just complied, partly because I liked gurneys. How fun is it when they lift you up really high and roll you down the hallway quickly like you're in the Kentucky Derby? Childish, I'm aware, but when you have no source of fun, you have to make your own. You take whatever you can get. That's how everyone should live their life every day.

Before all this happened, I would always wish to have things and go places that were perhaps out of reach. Fantastic things. I felt like happiness only occurs with new, exotic situations. In actuality, like a lot of people, I was misunderstanding the whole concept of happiness. Life's not about looking and searching to surround yourself with the things that you think will bring you joy, but it is about changing your attitude on happiness and using what is occurring in your life to make you happy. Perfect this attitude, and there is a way to an infinite amount of happiness.

So they rolled the gurney out the doors, into the cold, where snow was falling and whipping. Fear didn't particularly strike me, because my excitement was in the way. I mean, maybe this was the first real step towards my recovery. Whatever happens will happen.

It was just me in the back of the ambulance singing a song in my head and observing all the gizmos and gadgets they had in this one compared to the other one I had been in. Everything was pretty much the same. I was grateful nobody was using the gadgets and gizmos on me. I couldn't imagine someone using a defibrillator on me. The thought of it stung. After watching tree after snowy tree whip past the back window I could tell they stopped, based on the parking lot lights that I could see. Before I could finish my thought, I was whipped away from the ambulance, leaving it in the past. The trick is to move forward enough so you can actually move, but hold onto it enough to use whatever it is to become better.

They lifted me onto a bed that felt super comfy compared to the hard plastic and tight seatbelts on the gurney. The paramedics then left to go rescue the next person who needed them. A whole new set of faces came scurrying around like ants in a panic. I'm not completely sure if I was keeping my chill just because I felt like it or because my body was using all the energy I had to keep my heart thumping. I knew that they were killing my vibe. I wanted to sleep and I wanted calm and quiet. Is that too much to ask for? Instead I got them shouting and yelling at me, "Open your eyes!"

What was happening, as I found out later, was my lungs had filled up with fluid because my damaged heart valve was working so badly. My blood pressure had dropped to 65 over 20. That is really, really bad. Like near death. Normal is 120 over 80. The scene around me in the emergency room was a panic, my dad told me later, as he and my Uncle Doug watched in horror. The emergency room doctors were scrambling to get a line into one of my veins. They couldn't get one into my arms. They tried my groin. Finally they started poking my neck, because that's one of the last places to find an actual vein. My blood pressure was so low because my heart was too tired to keep working against the damaged heart valve. On about the eighth try it worked. They got a line into my neck. They started pumping medicine in me to get my heart going faster.

I was literally seconds away from having them use paddles on my chest to get my heart going. This was the second closest I came to dying, after the time the artery burst in my head back in Children's Hospital in Buffalo. After a couple hours I was stabilized. When they had originally done my brain surgery in Buffalo, they were hoping my heart valve would last another six months or a year, so I could get stronger before having heart surgery. No luck. It was obvious to the doctors that my heart valve wasn't going to make it, although they didn't tell me that right away.

This is when I turned on a mode of my body, which I call the ragdoll tactic. It's exactly what it sounds like. I let them do what they wished with me. It helps with the flinching factor when they go to stab in needle after needle. I let them stab me rapid fire with not just needles, but plastic ports in my neck, arm and groin. Every single one hurt more than a regular needle causing an excruciating pain.

A nurse came in and asked me if I needed anything. I said I was really thirsty, on a Sahara Desert level, and that my dad had a cup of water in his hand. But she said she was sorry and that she couldn't give me any. Nobody even took the time to explain the fact that I couldn't have water in case there was another emergency and they needed to put a breathing tube down my throat. I couldn't have anything in my stomach if that happened.

I decided if I had any measure of energy left, I wouldn't waste it fighting the powers controlling me. When in doubt, sleep. That is a philosophy to live by. You're happy and your thoughts are as clear as your nasal passage after a hot shower. For the first time in a long time, I was able to listen to my own philosophy. I put the fresh rubber oxygen nubbins in my nose and went to bed with no Keppra, no vomit, no elephant sitting on my chest. It was the first time I got a break since I left my house to go to the hospital.

A break is never really a break at a hospital. Always remember that. If there is a moment of calm, it is just anticipation for what craziness is going to erupt next.

CHAPTER SIXTEEN

Nothing by Mouth

My mom got back the next morning with my Aunt Paulette, who had come from her home in San Francisco to be by our side until everything was out of panic mode. My mom was panicky when she arrived but did a good job at trying to not let it show around me. Trust me, every mom would have had a panic level that was through the roof. My mom was really darn chill. I was still on NPO—which is short for nothing by mouth—until I had another pic line inserted. They needed to put that in so they could rush medication efficiently through my veins in case of emergency. But it was a minor operation, and I couldn't eat until it was performed.

I would constantly beg and plead every nurse I had for food or water. I was in so much distress that my nurse finally allowed me to have a one-inch square sponge, dipped in water, to be put in my mouth to keep it moist. I would be scolded if I started to suck all the water out of the sponge, but I did it anyway. This torture went on for three days. I swear an eternity fit into those three days. I never wanted anything that bad in my entire life. The hunger and thirst was so intense, that I was excited for the anesthesiologist to come in and give me the old KO. To keep me calm, everyone had to come in and tell me about the food I would get. The nurse even told me about a stash of popsicles in the freezer. I would have paid $45, maybe $50, to have a popsicle. Finally I was cleared for surgery, and all I could think of was that popsicle with my name on it in the freezer.

I was lying there on a hard table in a cold room with my right arm strapped down tight to an even colder, harder board. I saw my mom and dad from behind a glass window. The room was gray and looked as cold as it was. I waited patiently because I had to. I soon was asleep with a little help from modern medicine.

When I woke up, the staff rolled me out to see my mom and dad. They started to say how good I did.

"Can I have a popsicle now, pleaseee," I interrupted.

My mom and dad laughed and said, "We'll try."

"Please, I need one," I said. When we got to the room the nurse asked me what flavor I wanted. I went with the safe choice and said cherry.

Later the nurse came back and said, "We have orange or green." Ugh. Those flavors are to popsicles as black licorice is to candy, I thought. Beggars can't be choosers so I picked orange. It was the best popsicle I ever ate in my entire life. It is so true how absence makes the heart grow fonder. I know I'm dragging on about a popsicle, but this was a true lesson for me how lucky I am to have lived a life not having to wonder where my next meal was coming from. Up until this point, I never knew what it was like to be truly hungry. Why do some people have excess food and others have none? Why do some people have huge expensive houses and others barely have the clothes on their backs? Why did I survive a stroke when others died?

I really don't know, nor do I have the answers. But what I can do from here on out, is appreciate everything. Everything, even the tiniest things — the clean air you breathe, the warm house you live in. Everything you have, appreciate—even if it is the leaky faucet that keeps you up at night or the noisy radiator that wakes you up in the middle of the night. Well, heat is heat, and at least you know your water is running. Remember, when you start taking things for granted, you stop getting a full life experience.

CHAPTER SEVENTEEN

Nurse Nancy

The wheezy ache of my lungs became an unpleasant, familiar rhythm, like that of a sputtering car motor. Day by day, breathing became harder and harder. My lungs were submerged. Coughing up fluid became exhausting and really wasn't getting the job done. After a few days of a large plateau and more NPO periods, I met a nurse who stood out from the others. Her name was even made for a nurse: Nancy. We called her Nurse Nancy.

It takes an extra special person to become a nurse. It requires treating the person like they're family, by showing them extra care and compassion. It's also not just one of those jobs that ends when they walk out the automatic revolving door at the close of the day. It also means watching tragedy after tragedy but still having to keep a consistent type of attitude. I wouldn't dare to play a nurse in poker, because most have better "poker face smiles" than the professional gamblers. During my illness, nurse after nurse took me on like I was an adopted child. Not just Nancy and the Pittsburgh Children's Hospital nursing staff, but also at the Children's Institute and back home at the Children's Hospital of Buffalo. Thank God for them.

The biggest thing I learned from Nancy is to revolve your

life around something you love doing and show it by spreading that love everywhere. Nancy came in every day with a smile. She showed me love in everything she did. She told us she didn't even live in Pittsburgh. Interacting with Nurse Nancy, you would have never guessed that she had such a long commute through slippery snow-covered roads, arriving at 7 a.m., meaning she had to wake very early. One of the times when Nancy showed me her love was an evening in which I was feeling strong enough to want to sit up. So of course, with a lot of assistance, my mom and Nancy sat me in this plastic-covered chair. For the first time since all this started, while I was sitting in that chair, I actually felt a part of something, even if it was just my mom and Nurse Nancy's conversation. That feeling didn't last very long when the Lasix pill diuretic kicked in. (Dr. Orie said it makes you pee like a racehorse. Gosh, he wasn't exaggerating.)

I hated wearing diapers, but like I said before, when you gotta go, you gotta go. When I peed, it leaked out of the diaper and went right through my shorts, all over the chair and all over the floor. It was a terrible feeling. I felt pathetic, stupid, weak, infantile and most of all, like a burden. It felt like as soon as I started to feel the slightest bit good about myself, something would happen to gash my ego again. If egos could bleed, mine would have needed stitches. Nancy and my mom jumped right over and helped with damage control. I got back in bed feeling mad at myself that I even had to say, "I'm sorry I peed on your floor." Nancy and my mom could see this in my face. (I would never succeed as a poker player.) Emotional support is not exactly on the call of duty list for ICU nurses, but Nancy wasn't just any ICU nurse. She is Nurse Nancy.

Nancy told me there was nothing to be ashamed of. I was doing great and there are just some things we cannot control in this world. You can't control everything, but the way you react to everything makes all the difference. I could just lie there in bed moping about how horrible it feels to not be able to walk, stand, breathe, think, sleep, move or even smile normally, or I could get out of bed, tighten my diaper and work my ass off. (At 70 pounds, there was not much back there, so I'm talking figuratively.) After her pep talk, I was so ready to rock my next therapy session.

I met the therapy girls with a new-found enthusiasm. I walked to the nurses' stand feeling a sense of encouragement with every person I passed. I owned that bald head of mine. Each stride was not very big or steady. In fact, it was the complete opposite. My muscle control was still so weak it almost felt like there wasn't any muscle there at all. My frail bones were practically touching. I wanted to keep going so badly. I had the emotional heart in the game but the physical part of my heart just wasn't feeling it. Out of breath and exhausted, I had to throw in the towel.

People always idolize the idea of never giving up. This is where people misconceive this concept. Giving up is not always a bad thing. Nobody should ever do anything for the mere reason that they started it. If you lack passion, growth, strength, or even pleasure in whatever you're in the midst of, don't continue on because you can't "give up." People say things like, "How did you never give up?" I would tell them I did many times, but giving up doesn't mean that you can't take another road to the destination you want to arrive at. Sometimes it is necessary to throw in the towel for the time being. In many cases like mine, the universe rips the towel right of your hands and it is not your choice to make.

This was very present when an intense nurse barged into my room and yelled to my parents, "No more therapy today, since the surgery's tomorrow!" It was one of those moments where she totally pretended as if my ears were giving out instead of my heart.

I looked at my mom with a glance that said, "What a nut. She really has no idea what she's talking about."

My mom said, "Actually, there's something we've been meaning to tell you." Everyone knows, that is never a good thing. But after you hear it enough, it doesn't make your heart drop or fingers tremble like the first time someone says it to you. After finding out that I needed a heart-valve replacement, I was surprisingly happy. My mom said they waited to tell me so I didn't have to worry about anything longer than necessary. A hospital official who knew the terms and risk factors talked to me. My mom called in my favorite nurses to articulate the terms in a way that was easier to understand.

I had a choice between two replacement valves. Neither sounded that ideal. There was no true good way to put this. The mechanical valve sounded cooler than a pig valve. The pig valve also wouldn't last very long, meaning that they would have had to go back in to replace it every seven or eight years. I'd never want to go through anything like this again. The mechanical valve seemed like an obvious choice, because it was the only other choice. They told me I would be on a blood thinning tablet by mouth for the rest of my life if I choose that one.

Being the optimist I've always strived to be, I immediately said, "That's not that bad," and I chose that. The doctors' recommendation, given my situation, was that I get the mechanical valve. My mom came in choked-up. I would never be able to have children of my own if I chose the mechanical valve. Silence enveloped the room. I froze. Am I supposed to choose between the lives of my future children and my own life? I can't even decide what I want to eat for dinner.

I met the doctor who was going to perform the surgery. His name was Dr. Morell. He was very handsome and reassuring. I immediately nicknamed him Dr. Dreamy. He looked me in the eye and told me that after the surgery I was going to feel 5,000 times better.

CHAPTER EIGHTEEN
Finally, a Lucky Break

"Give it a good five minutes and Mr. Sandman will be here before you know it. I bet you don't know who that is." Those were the words of the anesthesiologist.

Of course, I know who that is, I thought. Do you think I live under a rock?

Talking to his crew of assistants and me, he said, "Do you guys remember that song? It was way before your ti …"

"Bum bum bum bum bum bum bum bum, bum bum bum bum bum," I started singing, "Mr. Sandman, bring me a dream!" Their mouths dropped as I burst out into *Mr. Sandman,* by The Chordettes. Everyone joined in as they rolled me down the hallway to the operating room. I fell asleep before we even reached our destination.

It's funny how what's meant to be really is meant to be. The surgeon came out of the operating room after only 90 minutes, compared with the three-to-four-hour estimate he had given us. My parents looked up. They didn't know if it was good news or bad. They didn't know if I was dead or alive. To die in the first 90 minutes wouldn't have made any sense. God used way too many of His wild cards to give up on me that easy. Dr. Morell told my parents he didn't achieve what he went in there to do — replace the valve — but instead he was able to sew and repair my valve! That meant that they wouldn't have to crack my breastbone open every couple of years to replace an artificial valve. I also would not have to take blood thinners every day for the rest of my life. And when the time comes, I could still have the chance to grant the earth with a little mini-me or two. This was a huge gift to me sent from God. I was still deep within a medically induced coma, so I didn't even get to throw in a woot-woot, which was a bummer.

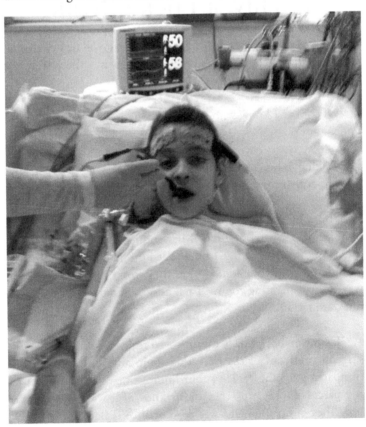

Waking up after a surgery is almost unexplainable because un-less you're a real-life sleeping beauty, sleep comes in one-night-at-a-time shifts. When you fall asleep you know what day it is. But when you wake up after surgery, it could be any number of days later. And if it's 20, you missed 20 days of your life (whoops). This time around, I only was under the day of and the day after surgery. Unlike when I had the craniotomy and was under eight straight days, this was just a very short, time-traveling catch-up.

I woke up and my mom filled me in with the great news. I was hoping Dr. Morell's words — 5,000 times better — would prove to be true soon. I had three painful, irritating and disgusting rub-ber tubes filled with pink liquid coming from my chest. They were there to drain fluid that the diuretics could not get out of my body. The PT women expected me to walk down the hall with a cane while the tubes were still in my chest. Using a safety pin attached to my diaper, we figured out a system to keep the tubes from get-ting tangled and tugging on the skin they were attached to. It was so challenging. But if a nurse was willing to hold that container of my disgusting pink lung juice as I walked down a hallway, I could at least give my all.

CHAPTER NINETEEN

Goodbye Keppra

After the initial pain and weakness wore off from the surgery, with a lot of sleep and a fair amount of narcotics, I started to feel better. The nursing staff recommended an EEG, so I could officially be taken off of Keppra, even though I hadn't taken it since the night before my ride to Pittsburgh Children's Hospital. Deep down I knew I didn't need it. Keeping me on it was another one of many precautionary measures. While I had taken it, I was throwing up almost every night, I had lost my appetite and I couldn't sleep the night. When my heart gave out, the doctors temporarily discontinued it. It was ten days since the last dosage and it was a full ten days of feeling good. The throwing up pretty much stopped all together. The EEG was not pleasant, I promise you. It consists of many wires being glued to your head with some ice-cold, sticky, smelly ointment. I'm pretty sure the guy used acetone to remove it. That really didn't seem like a good idea, considering I had a pretty fresh skull wound not too far away on my head.

But as they say, nothing worth anything is ever easy. The stress of the test was well worth it. Being off Keppra, combined with my heart being back on the rails to success, changed me into a new person. Not only was my appetite back, I slept at night and was alert during the day. It didn't take long for me to get out of the intensive care unit, because there was nothing left to really hold me back. I was walking 50 yards. Before the surgery I could barely take 50 steps.

After two liters of the pink liquid was drained out of my chest cavity, I was clear to have the tubes removed. Yes, I was trying to perform therapy before this with an equivalent of a party-sized soda bottle of pink lung juice in my chest cavity.

These repairs were game-changers. My appetite was back. I could concentrate. I was sleeping. I achieved a small amount of selective movement in my thumb. They discharged me from Pittsburgh Children's Hospital. I was reluctant to leave. The memories of the dark place I was in while I was at The Children's Institute haunted me. I was thinking about when my mom lay on the window sill while I threw up everything I ate and drank. Moments where catching my breath felt impossible. Staring at the huge adult-sized crib in the corner of my room. Nights when I lay counting each second until the sun would rise again. Life felt pretty good at the hospital. I just didn't want to endure the tortuous moments again.

When we arrived at the Institute, I wanted to surprise the staff. So I told my mom not to strap me in the wheelchair.

"I won't be sitting long," I said. I walked all the way from the front door, down the hallway, clapping my cane on the floor with what I thought was a sweet rhythm that mimicked Gene Wilder's scene in the original *Charlie and the Chocolate Factory* movie, where he walks to the gate to let the winners into the factory. It was the first true checkpoint of success. My smile felt so wide that I swear that numbness in my face disappeared, adding to the success of the moment. I FaceTimed the aunts and my concerned friends once I settled in.

I knew this wouldn't be like the time before. I could feel it, not just in my strength but in my spirit. I was still sleeping, breathing and eating, so the place was no longer a dreadful one. Instead, it was the place of opportunity, the one that made me cry tears of joy, hope and strength.

It was around Valentine's Day when we got back to the Institute. Before the surgery, my only friends were my mom, aunt and whoever came to visit me from back home. I was beyond excited when I came back and saw all new, higher-functioning potential friends. I saw a boy who looked like he was about my age also in a wheelchair and I said, "Hello."

He said, "F-you," in reply. Wow, tough crowd, I thought. Every time he rolled past me he gave me the middle finger. I later found out that he had a brain injury on the side that controls behavior. It made me thankful that my stroke and brain injuries hadn't affected the cognitive parts of my brain. I could think clearly.

When Dr. Morell told me I would feel 5,000 times better, I thought he was exaggerating. I thought he was just trying to make the situation feel not all negative. It turned out to be true in so many little ways, such as keeping eye contact with people, concentrating and remembering things. I don't remember realizing it got better. It just was better without notice. Dr. Morell did not exaggerate.

CHAPTER TWENTY

Little Superman

On Valentine's Day, the cutest, blue-eyed, brown-haired boy came up to me with encouragement from a therapist and handed me a Valentine and a piece of candy. I know how this sounds, but I am telling you it's not what you think. I remember it clearly. The card read, "Bee my Valentine," with a picture of a bee and the words "buzz, buzz." In all uppercase letters it read: "FROM GABE." Gabe was six. Yeah, not exactly *The Fault in Our Stars* material, but it was the beginning of a beautiful friendship. He wore Superman pajamas every day, with a cape. Once he knew my name, he would call me in the hallways, saying, "Mar-ee-on-ah." Gabe was the first real friend that I made since I got sick.

I helped him in his therapy by telling him, "If you want to be Superman, you need to be able to walk." I would cheer him on every time he did something good. I met him at the top of the therapy stairs with a high five. We played Wii. Well, we turned the controllers on and made Mario run around in circles. It didn't feel like I was spending my time keeping a kindergartener busy.

After we were settled into our room, they told us they were giving me a roommate. They took out the huge baby cage and put in a bed on the other side of the room. I had never had a roommate before. I sure hope she's nice, I thought. The people at the Institute liked me. I'm pretty sure they wouldn't let me down. They didn't at all. Marissa was two years older than me. She was super friendly and nice to me. She had RND, which is a painful nerve disorder, so our therapies never really overlapped. She quickly became my friend. We would laugh at the creepy nurses together and talk about our favorite TV shows. Her mom would talk to my mom and bring her food. I know my mom appreciated this a lot because before Marissa came, the only people she had to talk to was the medical staff, Aunt Paulette and me.

Marissa and Gabe were my true friends. They saw me for me, not the bald skeleton that I had become. I was kind of a scary sight. They never looked at me as anything unusual. I was just simply their friend. They taught me a lot about friendship. It's not about making friends with the coolest, most popular, best-looking person. It's about seeing people for what they have, not what they're missing.

CHAPTER TWENTY-ONE

When Life Hands You a Stroke

The improvements were endless, once my mitral valve no longer resembled a piece of swiss cheese. My endurance was better because everything else was better. I started to leave the cane in my room when we went for walks down the hallway. We ventured out to the mall more often, after I started getting day passes from the Institute to do so. It was all upwards from there. Gabe and Marissa went home before I did. It is a tradition at the Children's Institute to paint a ceiling tile that gets put up in one of the rooms when you're discharged. Past patients covered theirs with quotes such as, "Don't tell me the sky's the limit when there are footprints on the moon." Another was, "Life's not waiting for the storm to pass. It's learning how to dance in the rain." Others just had pictures or initials of whatever was important to them.

I watched Gabe as he painted his favorite color and a few safari animals. I asked him if he was excited to go home. Gabe and his mother told me he didn't want to go home because at the Institute he could ride a bike inside.

"My mom never lets me ride a bike inside at home," he said.

"I know," I said with a smile, "my mom doesn't let me do that either." Perspective is everything.

Gabe didn't leave without saying goodbye. "Mar-ee-on-ah!" he yelled. "Here, I picked this out. It's my favorite color so you don't forget me," he told me as he handed me a red bracelet with a silver star. Gabe gave me much more than just a bracelet that winter. He was motivation, positivity, hope and optimism all packed in to one unforgettable, tiny person.

The goodbye was truly bittersweet. I was going to miss my superhero sidekick. At the same time, I was happy God even gave me one. How many people get to say they're friends with a six-year-old superhero who beat a life-threatening illness? Who also helped you to save the world against negative attitudes? ... Exactly.

Therapy was a superb series of sky-rocketing, rapidly occurring improvements. It was not long after Gabe left that it was my turn to make my tile and prepare to return home. My tile had to be great. It couldn't be just some cliché. The tile was a big deal to me. It will be there, hopefully, as long as the building is still standing. It will leave a mark that I went through there, just like the many before me, and came out stronger. It needed to be specific enough that it would fully represent my struggle. Looking back at everything, it didn't feel as horrible as it actually was.

Optimism is always key, no matter what is going on. Lucky for me the word "stroke" doesn't always have to mean just a glitch in your arteries that changes lives forever. It could also be used as a play on words to represent something positively life-changing. I obtained so much more on my journey than I lost. This is all because of that one key word, optimism. A huge saying that represents optimism is, "When life hands you lemons, make lemonade." This phrase like many motivational ones, is overused and has become a cliché. Using the creative gift that God has blessed me with, I put a spin on it. The phrase I put on my ceiling tile represented my optimism. "When life hands you a stroke, paint a picture." That is exactly what I did. Initially when I was told that statistically it is more common to win the lottery than to obtain the illness that I had, like anyone would be, I was upset and confused. Why this? Why me? Why not the lottery? I asked myself.

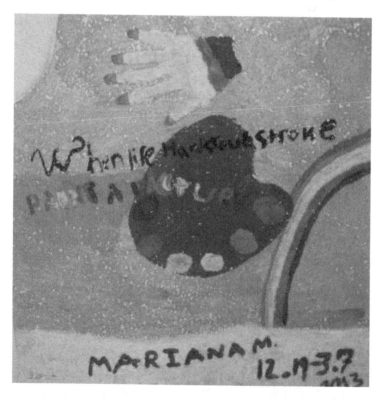

I wouldn't, even if it was possible, trade this experience for any sum of money. I've come out of this experience with so much more than money can buy. I've learned something that some people never learn in a lifetime.

CHAPTER TWENTY-TWO
Here Comes the Sun

I thought my days of insomnia were left behind at the cardiac ICU, but as my final days at the Children's Institute were winding down, the excitement that filled my entire body kept me awake. Obviously I preferred this insomnia over the kind where I couldn't sleep because I couldn't breathe.

My dad let my mom go sleep at the hotel close by that night. I asked my dad if he could come talk to me to help me shake a few nerves off so I could finally get to sleep. Of course he said yes and pulled a chair over.

I told him something like, "I'm excited to go home. I prayed for it every day since I left, but what if I don't have any friends when I get back?"

"That's the least of your worries, the hard part is over," he said.

I replied, "Like that one Beatles song?" Then on cue, we both started singing, *Here Comes the Sun*. This was the moment that made me realize I was truly lucky, I had two amazing fathers in my lifetime. I had an entire family that loved me.

CHAPTER TWENTY-THREE

Home

The morning of my departure had a surreal feeling. Ever since that very first day I woke up with the needle feeling in my throat, everything felt like a lucid nightmare I couldn't escape. I floated through each day accepting it all. Now it was time to finally wake up and return to the uncensored world. My family packed everything up and loaded it into the car. The drive home felt long, even though 210 minutes is nothing compared to the countless hours that I spent anticipating the very moment of walking through my door.

Even driving by familiar places I considered close to home provoked a joy in me that really couldn't be substituted anywhere but home. I thought about every change that occurred since my feet stepped out of the front door of my house. I had no idea that I was leaving for more than an afternoon, let alone 150 days! Will it be different to sit in my room? Will the hair-straightener work that I can't use? Or what about the high-heel shoes that I can't wear? Will I be haunted by every ability that I lost?

Finally we turned onto my street, and my family blasted, *Here Comes the Sun* on our car radio. This was a moment that had absolutely no guarantees, no promises. God helped me beat the odds, beyond any scientific percentage. I walked up my driveway, which has an incline. I was no longer Gene Wilder as Willy Wonka, I was Rocky climbing the stairs.

With God, anything is possible!

ACKNOWLEDGEMENTS

I have always known that I wanted to become a writer. I would like to thank my dad, Mark Gaughan, for being so influential in never letting that dream die.

Without my team of aunts that made my force field complete, I would not have survived. Thanks to Aunt Lisa for helping me keep a strong faith in God. Thanks to Aunt Paulette and Uncle Doug, who gave up their lives for a year to come and support and motivate me in a long, difficult recovery. Cousin Rachelle helped make their visits possible. Thanks to Aunt Jen for saving my life, not just once but numerous times.

Thanks Mom, for never giving up on me and staying by my side every step of the way. Thanks also to everyone behind the scenes for your support and prayers. (See, they paid off.)

Thanks to every doctor and nurse who cared for me and who work their butts off every day for their patients. Their dedication goes way beyond anything learned in medical school.

I appreciate all my family and friends for listening, saving and recording any media event that I am involved with. Here's to you, support team. Thanks for being the size of a small country.

A special thanks to Sarah Fallica, the social worker who recommended me to the Make-A-Wish Foundation. Thank you to Make-A-Wish for allowing children in great need to realize that a wonderful wish can come true. In particular, I got to work with two great Make-A-Wish volunteers, Marianne Tyree and Frank Browning.

I was lucky to work with a swag group of people who made the publishing of this book possible, my editor and publisher Darcy Thiel and her team of Mark Krawczyk, Karen Sharp-Price and Sallie Randolph. Thank you all for your expertise and guidance.